weird but true!

HALLOWEEN

NATIONAL
GEOGRAPHIC
KiDS

weird but true!

HALLOWEEN

300 SPOOKY FACTS TO SCARE YOU SILLY

NATIONAL GEOGRAPHIC
WASHINGTON, D.C.

You can buy a
cat costume
for your dog
or a
dog costume
for your cat.

A **pumpkin** is the
most popular
pet costume in the United States.

Is this a trick or a treat?

THE BOMBAY is the only cat breed that is always **PURELY BLACK.**

In the United States, **75 percent** of households hand out **Halloween candy,** according to a survey.

In Germany, it's considered
GOOD LUCK
if a
BLACK
CAT
crosses your path
from right to left.

A theme park
in St. Louis, Missouri, U.S.A., held a
"COFFIN CHALLENGE"
in which a contestant could win $300 if they
LAY IN A COFFIN FOR 30 HOURS.

Legend says that if a **BAT FLIES INTO YOUR HOUSE** ON HALLOWEEN, your home will be **HAUNTED.**

A corn maze IN IDAHO, U.S.A., WAS DESIGNED TO LOOK LIKE A **Pac-Man game.**

A Philadelphia Flyers fan **carved a pumpkin** to look like the hockey team's **giant orange mascot,** Gritty.

11

STONE GARGOYLES on the **NOTRE DAME CATHEDRAL** in Paris, France, were built to **PROTECT** the building from **BAD SPIRITS.**

Ghost peppers are so spicy that some are **400 times hotter** than a **jalapeño!**

A **"fall fairy"** made from cornstalks won first place in a **scarecrow contest** in Homewood, Illinois, U.S.A.

A
tarantula's
venom
is weaker
than the venom
in a typical
BEE STING.

Tarantulas **don't spin webs,** but sometimes they **MAKE A TRIP WIRE** that acts as an alert if something comes into their burrow.

Bumba lennoni, a type of tarantula, is named after the **BEATLES MUSICIAN** John Lennon.

15

In the early 1900s, **Halloween** was associated with **romance** and **love.**

Cupid symbols were included in Halloween festivities to **encourage** romance.

A survey found that **46.8 percent** of people **believe** that you should **EAT** a candy corn whole, **NOT** in sections.

START!

But when **EATING candy corn** by colored section, most people **START** with **WHITE.**

Gummy tarantulas the size of a **kid's hand** come in lime, cherry, and grape flavors.

With a

DARK UPPER SHELL,

A BRIGHT ORANGE BODY,

AND PURPLE CLAWS,

**Halloween crabs look
dressed for the occasion.**

Where's the party?

The actress who voices **PRINCESS ANNA** in the movie ***FROZEN*** was asked by her daughter to dress up as **ANNA'S SISTER, ELSA,** for Halloween.

"Goblin" is related to the German word **kobold,** a household spirit who **throws tantrums.**

TELLING **GHOST STORIES** WAS A CHRISTMAS EVE TRADITION IN 19TH-CENTURY ENGLAND.

A mom in Ohio, U.S.A., makes her kids' **Halloween costumes** entirely out of **crocheted yarn.**

A HUNGARIAN **PULI,** with its **LONG** and **ROPY HAIR,** went as a

MOP in a **HALLOWEEN PARADE** in Kentucky, U.S.A.

THE world's largest JACK-O'-LANTERN weighed 1,810 pounds— (821 kg) MORE THAN TWO SIBERIAN TIGERS.

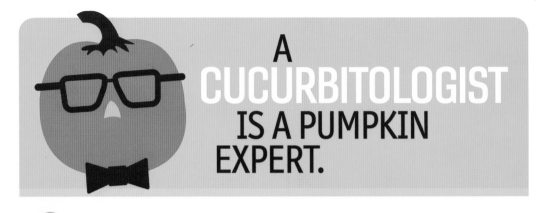

A **CUCURBITOLOGIST** IS A PUMPKIN EXPERT.

One man bobbed for 37 apples in one minute— the world record.

Pee-yew!

PUMPKIN BUGS, a kind of STINKBUG, releases a FOUL SMELL as a type of self-defense.

25

In 1924, **HALLOWEEN PRANKSTERS** turned the **POWER OFF** throughout the city of Riverside, Illinois, U.S.A.

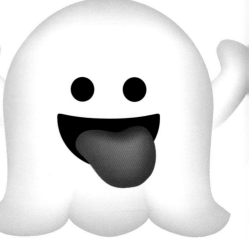

There are more HALLOWEEN EMOJIS than there are U.S. STATES.

You can buy peppermint-flavored candy corn at Christmastime.

The world's largest haystack, made in the Netherlands, was **three stories tall** and **56 feet wide.** (17 m)

People in Utah listen to more **HALLOWEEN PLAYLISTS** than people in any other U.S. state, a survey found.

An artist in Kentucky, U.S.A., turns hay bales into **3D ART PIECES** for Halloween.

PUMPKINS FLOAT.

Pumpkins are 90 PERCENT WATER.

At a **FLOATING PUMPKIN PATCH** in Northern California, U.S.A., you can swim in a pool to **PICK OUT YOUR PUMPKIN.**

THE VAMPIRE BAT bites livestock and uses its straw-shaped tongue to **DRINK THE BLOOD.**

The bat has special **HEAT SENSORS** on its **NOSE** that help find the **BEST SPOT TO BITE.**

Scientists are studying **TARANTULA VENOM** to make a new type of **PAINKILLER.**

The **BLACK, ORANGE, and WHITE** markings on the Halloween snake warn predators that it is **HIGHLY VENOMOUS.**

Ssssstay away!

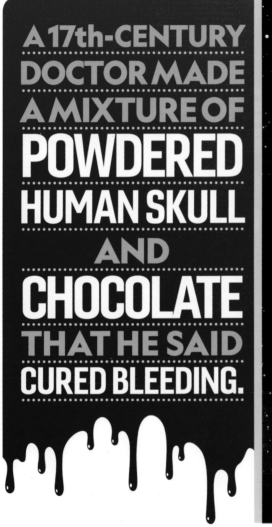

A 17th-CENTURY DOCTOR MADE A MIXTURE OF **POWDERED HUMAN SKULL** AND **CHOCOLATE** THAT HE SAID **CURED BLEEDING.**

THE SKULL NEBULA, in the constellation Cetus, was first discovered IN 1785.

35

A Los Angeles artist turned her parents' home **into a** fanged, eight-eyed monster **for** Halloween.

A man from Washington State, U.S.A., made a working **VIDEO GAME** out of a **PUMPKIN** in which the stem acted as the **JOYSTICK.**

Lanterns made from **turnips** and **pumpkins** were lit to ward off **evil spirits** in Scotland and Ireland.

Special "undertaker" ants remove dead ants from their colonies.

Mary Shelley wrote *Frankenstein* when she was a teenager.

In the book, Frankenstein is the name of the scientist, not the monster.

OCTOBER 30 IS

National Candy Corn Day **IN THE UNITED STATES.**

Known as the "**witches of Subeshi,**" mummies more than 2,000 years old were found in western China wearing **POINTY BLACK HATS.**

The
QUEENS' BEDROOM,
which contains President Andrew Jackson's bed, is said to be one of the most
HAUNTED
spots in the White House.

At the annual
Tompkins Square
Halloween
Dog Parade in New York City,
participants have included a
dog dressed as "Amelia Doghart"
and another dressed as King Tut.

43

Nicknamed **SKELETORUS,** a kind of peacock spider from Australia has a **BLACK BODY** with **WHITE STRIPES.**

It does a **FANCY DANCE** to attract a mate.

THE LOUDEST SCREAM ever recorded **MEASURED 129 DECIBELS—** that's as loud as a **JET AT TAKEOFF.**

FOR HALLOWEEN, ONE U.S. AIRLINE JOKED THAT IT FLEW ACROSS THE COUNTRY FROM **"GHOST TO GHOST."**

In 1999,
25 SKYDIVERS,
each dressed
as the monster from
FRANKENSTEIN,
parachuted onto
a baseball field in
Frankenstein,
Missouri,
U.S.A.

Dragon's House of Horrors, the **WORLD'S LONGEST INDOOR HAUNTED HOUSE,** in **New Mexico, U.S.A.,** is more than **A MILE LONG.**
(1.6 km)

In 2016, a **GHOSTLY LOOKING WHITE OCTOPUS** was spotted off the coast of Hawaii, U.S.A.

The web of a DARWIN'S BARK SPIDER can stretch more than 80 FEET ACROSS A RIVER.

(25 M)

Two California, U.S.A., teens made an **eight-foot-tall** (2.4-m) **animatronic dragon** that **breathed real fire** for Halloween.

American colonists **cut off the top of pumpkins,** scooped out the insides, and filled them with **spices, honey, and milk** to make an early version of **pumpkin pie.**

YOU CAN BUY A SKULL-SHAPED CAKE PAN.

IT WAS THOUGHT THAT ON HALLOWEEN NIGHT IN NORFOLK, ENGLAND, **ELVES WOULD RIDE** ON THE BACKS OF **CATS.**

Independence, Kansas, U.S.A., holds a NEEWOLLAH festival— **THAT'S "HALLOWEEN" SPELLED BACKWARD—** to encourage kids to have fun without **PLAYING PRANKS.**

GHOST-FACED BATS

get their name from their ghoulish look— **THEIR TINY EYES** appear to be **INSIDE THEIR LARGE EARS.**

HALLOWEEN BOWLING = ROLLING PUMPKINS INTO "GHOST PINS"

53

Thousands of Americans signed a petition to **OFFICIALLY MOVE** Halloween to the **last Saturday** of October.

The U.S. Department of Defense has a **zombie apocalypse** plan.

(Don't worry. It was created as a military training exercise.)

On Halloween, people have **SPENT THE NIGHT** in Romania's Bran Castle, where author **Bram Stoker** took inspiration for his book *DRACULA.*

Skeleton sledding, an Olympic sport in which riders race down an icy track **headfirst,** reportedly got its name because the sled has a **bony appearance.**

MOVIEGOERS CAN WATCH FILMS ON AN OUTDOOR SCREEN AT HOLLYWOOD FOREVER CEMETERY IN LOS ANGELES, CALIFORNIA.

A company created candy **gummy eyeballs** just for Halloween.

Guests wander among more than **7,000 illuminated pumpkins** at Van Cortlandt Manor in Croton-on-Hudson, New York, U.S.A., during the **Great Jack O'Lantern Blaze.**

Installations include a working **doomsday grandfather clock** and a **circus train.**

Illinois harvests more than 300 MILLION POUNDS (136 million kg) **of pumpkins EVERY YEAR, the most of any U.S. state.**

TO CURE **BLOOD DISEASES,** A 17TH-CENTURY RECIPE DESCRIBES HOW TO **COOK BLOOD** INTO **MARMALADE.**

In **Arabic** mythology, **ghouls** were **monsters** that haunted graveyards.

Fans sent **candy** to **Peanuts cartoonist Charles Schulz** after *It's the Great Pumpkin, Charlie Brown* first aired because they felt bad that Charlie Brown **got rocks instead of candy.**

On Halloween night, Austrians leave out **BREAD AND WATER AS A SNACK** for the returning souls of **DEAD RELATIVES.**

An **ASTEROID** that **LOOKED LIKE A SKULL** passed by Earth on Halloween in 2015.

PEOPLE ON THE ITALIAN ISLAND OF SARDINIA CALL THE PUMPKINS THEY CARVE FOR HALLOWEEN *CONCAS DE MORTU:* "HEADS OF THE DEAD."

In 2018, Halloween paradegoers in Kawasaki, Japan, **dressed up as** famous paintings.

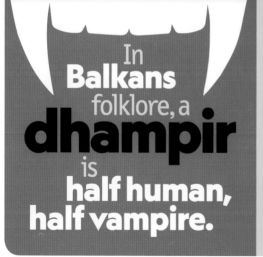

In **Balkans** folklore, a **dhampir** is **half human, half vampire.**

Americans send 21 million Halloween cards every year.

XOXOOOOO

THE *QUEEN MARY*, a former luxury ocean liner, is said to be one of the **MOST HAUNTED**

places in the United States,
      with ghost sightings of
   a **SAILOR** and a **LADY IN WHITE.**

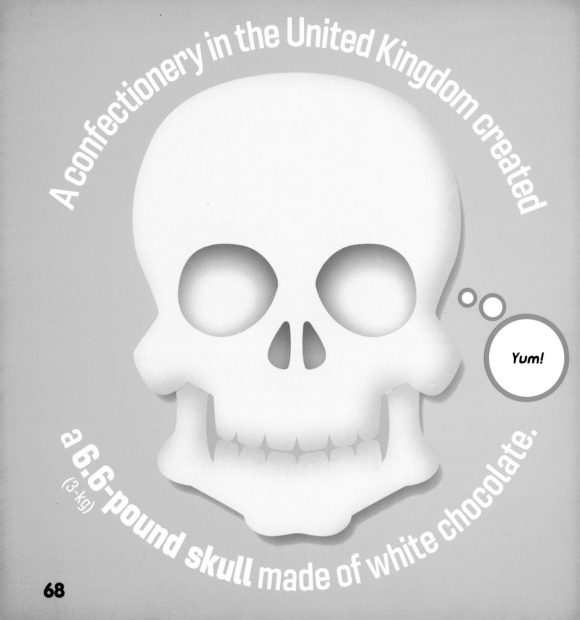

A confectionery in the United Kingdom created a **6.6-pound** (3-kg) **skull** made of white chocolate.

Yum!

In some parts of the United States, the **NIGHT BEFORE HALLOWEEN** is known as **MISCHIEF NIGHT,** when **PEOPLE PULL PRANKS.**

The leaves of **GHOST PLANTS** have a powdery coating that makes them look **WHITE.**

A survey found that **81 PERCENT** of **PARENTS** admit to **STEALING** some of their kids' **HALLOWEEN CANDY.**

And **26 PERCENT SNEAK THE CANDY** after their **KIDS ARE IN BED** or when they're at school.

The most common ghost sighting in the White House is of Abraham Lincoln.

One fast-food restaurant sold a **"Scary Black Cherry"** slushie at Halloween time that made people's **tongues turn black.**

Experts aren't sure **WHY WITCHES** are shown wearing **POINTY HATS;** in the Middle Ages, witches were often drawn **WITHOUT HATS.**

A company made "werewolf fur" cotton candy.

Halfway through their growing season,

giant pumpkins

can increase by 60 pounds
(27 kg)
a day.

403 kg

It can take a
giant pumpkin
more than
100 days
to reach
full size.

THE WEEK BEFORE HALLOWEEN IN 2012, A FISHERMAN FROM SALEM, MASSACHUSETTS, U.S.A., CAUGHT A

BLACK-AND-ORANGE LOBSTER,

NOW ON DISPLAY AT THE NEW ENGLAND AQUARIUM.

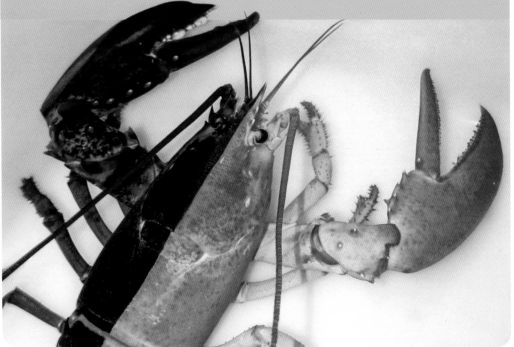

A **teal-colored pumpkin** outside a house on Halloween means nonfood items are available for kids who **have food allergies.**

HALLOWEEN has been CELEBRATED for about 2,000 YEARS.

You can buy a 26-INCH-LONG (66-cm) GUMMY WORM.

The average **trick-or-treater** takes home the equivalent of **three cups** of **sugar** on **Halloween.** (710 mL)

The Louisiana Purchase,
which added 828,000 square miles
of land to the United States, *(2.14 million sq km)*
was finalized on
October 31, 1803.

A **HAUNTED HOUSE** near Atlanta, Georgia, U.S.A., is said to be **SO SCARY** that people with **HEART CONDITIONS** are warned against entering it.

"Dord" is a **ghost word—** it was **in a dictionary** even though it isn't a real word.

Travelers in ancient Ireland carried KNIVES or NEEDLES on Halloween to protect against FAIRIES.

"MONSTER RAP" IS THE RAP VERSION OF THE HIT HALLOWEEN SONG "MONSTER MASH."

To make the sound of a casket opening in "Monster Mash," a musician pulled a nail across a wooden slab.

You can make edible **pumpkin-flavored** play dough.

AT A
SKELETON MUSEUM
IN OKLAHOMA CITY, OKLAHOMA, U.S.A.,
FLESH-EATING BEETLES
ARE USED TO **CLEAN THE BONES.**

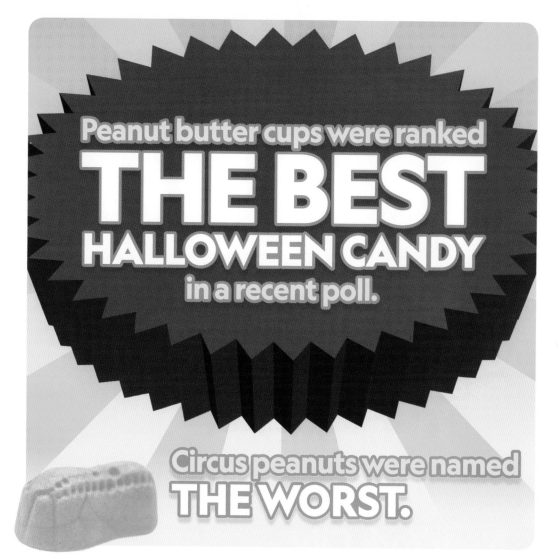

Peanut butter cups were ranked **THE BEST** HALLOWEEN CANDY in a recent poll.

Circus peanuts were named **THE WORST.**

Two million spectators watch **60,000** costumed paradegoers in the annual **Village Halloween Parade** in **New York City.**

The town of **Keene,** New Hampshire, U.S.A., **set a record** for lighting **30,581** jack-o'-lanterns.

Jolly Ranchers

ARE THE most popular Halloween candy IN UTAH, U.S.A., A SURVEY FOUND.

In Scotland, around Halloween, people traditionally PEELED APPLES into ONE LONG STRIP and tossed the peel over their shoulder.

THE LETTER that the peel formed was said to be the first initial of THE PERSON'S FUTURE LOVE.

HARRY POTTER got his LIGHTNING-BOLT SCAR on **HALLOWEEN.**

On Halloween in parts of northern England, people used to **TAKE OFF THEIR NEIGHBORS' FRONT DOORS** and **HIDE THEM.**

YOU CAN BUY GUMMY DRACULA FANGS.

The aerial view of a **corn maze** in Wisconsin, U.S.A., revealed **narwhals, unicorns,** and **ninja cats.**

A legend from the early 1900s held that if you **walked backward in the moonlight on Halloween,** the face of your **true love would appear in a mirror.**

DRY ICE, used to make decorations like **WITCHES' CAULDRONS** bubble, is frozen **CARBON DIOXIDE.**

In 1699, a man who bought two **ANCIENT EGYPTIAN MUMMIES** was reportedly **HAUNTED** by two ghosts.

Once he **GOT RID OF** the mummies, the ghosts reportedly **DISAPPEARED.**

BONFIRES lit during **EARLY HALLOWEEN** celebrations were thought to keep **EVIL SPIRITS AWAY.**

A SEED FROM WHAT WAS ONCE THE **WORLD'S HEAVIEST PUMPKIN** SOLD FOR **$1,600** IN 2016.

A group of people in London, England, set a world record by wrapping **51 INDIVIDUALS IN TOILET PAPER** as **"MUMMIES"** in three minutes.

Mummy, is that you?

The oldest known wrapped mummy lived more than **7,000 YEARS AGO.**

97

NASA named a nebula— a cloud of gas and dust in outer space— WITCH HEAD because it looked like A WITCH SCREAMING.

On Halloween night, according to one legend, you might **SEE A WITCH** if you put your clothes on inside out and walk backward.

FOR HALLOWEEN, A FORMER MAYOR IN WEST VIRGINIA, U.S.A., DECORATES HIS HOME WITH **3,000 CARVED PUMPKINS.**

Some
31 MILLION
Americans will
DRESS UP
THEIR PETS
on Halloween.

In Germany, it's a **TRADITION** to **HIDE ALL THE KNIVES ON HALLOWEEN** so any returning spirits **ARE NOT HARMED.**

SNAIL ZOMBIES are snails whose tentacles have been taken over by **PARASITIC WORMS.**

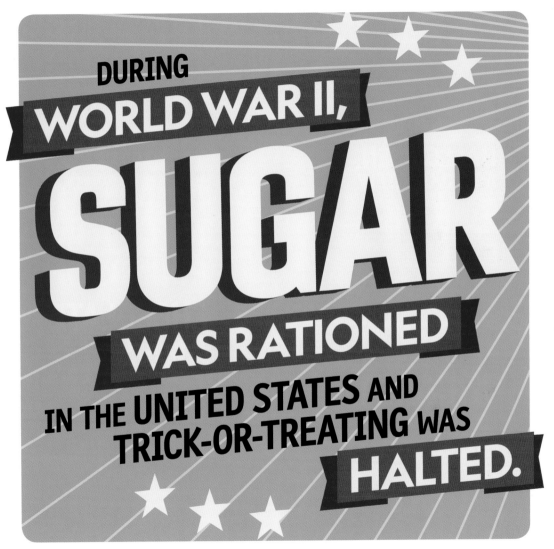

DURING WORLD WAR II, SUGAR WAS RATIONED IN THE UNITED STATES AND TRICK-OR-TREATING WAS HALTED.

EVERY HALLOWEEN, APPROXIMATELY

600 MILLION POUNDS

(272 MILLION KG)

OF CANDY ARE SOLD IN THE UNITED STATES.

ABOUT NINETY MILLION POUNDS OF

(41 MILLION KG)

CHOCOLATE ARE SOLD THE WEEK OF HALLOWEEN.

Good for him. Bad for me.

A man from Jamaica, New York, U.S.A., smashed **31 PUMPKINS** with a sledgehammer in one minute.

A local chef used the **PUMPKIN REMAINS** to make pumpkin pies.

The writer **WASHINGTON IRVING** used real people's names for the characters in **"THE LEGEND OF SLEEPY HOLLOW"**– and you can visit some of their graves.

CLOWN COSTUMES CAN **SCARE** KIDS SO MUCH THAT SOME PLACES HAVE **BANNED** THEM DURING HALLOWEEN.

IN THE 19TH-CENTURY UNITED STATES, PEOPLE **PICNICKED IN CEMETERIES.**

SILLY STRING IS BANNED in Hollywood, California, U.S.A., on Halloween.

Halloween's **ORANGE-AND-BLACK** color theme symbolizes harvest season, summer's end, and **DEATH.**

Sigh. No pumpkin patch for me this year.

PUMPKINS ARE GROWN ON EVERY CONTINENT EXCEPT ANTARCTICA.

One of the first
WEREWOLF STORIES
was written by a Roman author nearly
2,000 YEARS AGO.

After **King Tut's tomb was opened** in 1922, some people believed that the mummy **put a curse** on the explorers who had disturbed it.

Howard Carter, the archaeologist who **discovered** the tomb, gave a friend a paperweight of a mummified hand— then the friend's **house burned down.**

A **radiologist** who supposedly x-rayed the mummy **died soon afterward.**

On Halloween, a couple dressed as **Luke Skywalker** and **Princess Leia** rode through New York City streets on a replica speeder bike that was made to look like it was levitating.

In the Harry Potter book series, a

DEATHDAY PARTY

is a celebration that ghosts throw in honor of the day they died.

In October 2010, more than **4,000 PEOPLE** dressed as

ZOMBIES

"INVADED" Asbury Park, New Jersey, U.S.A.

IN BRITAIN IN THE 1600S, "JACK-O'-LANTERN" REFERRED TO A NIGHT WATCHMAN CARRYING A LANTERN.

If you **SEE A SPIDER** on Halloween night, it means that the spirit of a **DECEASED LOVED ONE IS LOOKING OUT FOR YOU,** according to a superstition.

PRESIDENT Jimmy Carter's daughter had a **HALLOWEEN-THEMED BIRTHDAY PARTY** at the White House.

In Belleville, Illinois, U.S.A., it's illegal to go trick-or-treating if you are more than 12 years old.

A jumping spider from East Africa **craves mosquitoes filled with human blood.**

Feed me!

Halloween has been called **Nut Crack Night,** when chestnuts were roasted to foretell a **good love match.**

An orange rock formation called **Pumpkin Spring** in Grand Canyon National Park, U.S.A., looks **just like** a **hollowed-out pumpkin.**

American pioneers celebrated **Halloween** with **corn-popping** parties.

A dwarf planet on THE EDGE OF THE SOLAR SYSTEM is nicknamed "**THE GOBLIN.**"

IT'S ESTIMATED THAT FEWER THAN 10 PERCENT OF THE **MILLIONS OF PUMPKINS** GROWN IN THE UNITED KINGDOM ARE EATEN.

CHINA GROWS SIX TIMES MORE PUMPKINS AND GOURDS THAN THE UNITED STATES.

Nearly
18 PERCENT
of Americans said
THEY HAVE BEEN
IN THE PRESENCE
of a **GHOST,**
a survey found.

Another survey
found that
33 PERCENT
of people are willing to
LIVE IN A HAUNTED
HOUSE.

At an annual **PUMPKIN REGATTA** near Sacramento, California, U.S.A., people paddle across a lake in **HOLLOWED-OUT PUMPKINS.**

There are more kids of

TRICK-OR-TREAT AGE

in the United States
than the

**POPULATION
OF CANADA.**

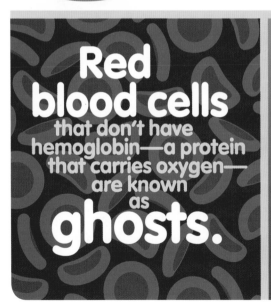

**Red
blood cells**
that don't have
hemoglobin—a protein
that carries oxygen—
are known
as
ghosts.

A farmer in
California, U.S.A., used
plastic molds to grow
"PUMPKINSTEINS"—
pumpkins in the
shape of Frankenstein's
monster.

White House Halloween

FLORAL DECORATIONS

were made to look like President

BARACK OBAMA'S DOGS

Sunny and Bo dressed as a sunflower and a pirate.

WOLVES DON'T HOWL AT THE FULL MOON—

they howl as a call to hunt.

In 2017, a baby with the **last name Frankenstein** was **born on Halloween** in Florida, U.S.A.

MAGICIAN AND ESCAPE ARTIST **HARRY HOUDINI** DIED ON HALLOWEEN.

SOME 1,300 PEOPLE **LIVE** IN TOMBSTONE, ARIZONA, U.S.A.

One man in Peru has **THE LARGEST COLLECTION** of candy wrappers: **MORE THAN 5,000!**

FIRE TRUCKS in SLEEPY HOLLOW, New York, U.S.A., have an image of the **HEADLESS HORSEMAN** on their doors.

Orb-weaver spiders eat their own webs TO RECYCLE the silk.

For Halloween, **M&M'S** introduced **cookies-and-"screeem"**-flavored candies.

In 2018, more than
SEVEN MILLION U.S. ADULTS
DRESSED AS A WITCH FOR HALLOWEEN—
that's more than the population of Colorado.

A crater on WIZARD

ISLAND in the middle of Crater Lake in Oregon, U.S.A., is called the **WITCHES CAULDRON.**

Historians think trick-or-treating came from **"MUMMING,"** when people would **DRESS UP AND DANCE FOR TREATS.**

In **SCOTLAND, TRICK-OR-TREATING** is known as **GUISING.**

The Klown Doll Museum in Plainview, Nebraska, U.S.A., is home to more than **7,000 clown dolls.**

A Canadian dad made Halloween costumes out of cardboard that **allowed his kids to transform from cars to robots.**

During October in **ALBUQUERQUE, NEW MEXICO,** U.S.A., you can go on a three-hour **NIGHTTIME BICYCLE TOUR** to historical places said to be **HAUNTED.**

You can buy a **PACIFIER** that makes a **BABY** appear to have **VAMPIRE TEETH.**

If you get stuck in one **CORN MAZE** in Floral Park, New York, U.S.A., you can **CALL FOR HELP** on a corn-stylized phone.

PART OF **THE FILLING IN KIT KAT** BARS IS MADE FROM **GROUND-UP KIT KATS.**

Just for Halloween, **KIT KATS** come in **GLOW-IN-THE-DARK** wrappers.

The largest temporary **CORN MAZE,** located in California, U.S.A., was **AS BIG AS 45 FOOTBALL FIELDS.**

In 1764, a mysterious animal known as the **Beast of Gévaudan**

terrorized southern France and inspired many werewolf legends.

In addition to werewolves, ancient stories feature **werefoxes, weretigers, and werehyenas.**

In the 1984 movie *Ghostbusters*, **SHAVING CREAM** was used when the Stay Puft Marshmallow Man **EXPLODED.**

PART OF THE ROOF OF A BUILDING IN WINDBER, PENNSYLVANIA, U.S.A., IS A GIANT **OUIJA BOARD.**

FULL MOONS HAVE OCCURRED ON HALLOWEEN ONLY FOUR TIMES SINCE 1950— IN 1955, 1974, 2001, AND 2020.

Originally, **turnips,** not pumpkins, were **carved** for Halloween.

Less than **5 percent** of the animal species on Earth have a skeleton **made of bones.**

That's weird!

According to legend, the **GHOST OF A CAT** lives in the basement of the **U.S. CAPITOL BUILDING** and **APPEARS BEFORE HISTORIC EVENTS.**

In 2005, the New Orleans Vampire Association **was formed to provide support for people who self-identify as** vampires.

People can fish for pumpkinseed **sunfish** in **Witch Lake** in Marquette County, Michigan, U.S.A.

A café in Himeji, Japan, is devoted to **black cats.**

Black tea, anyone?

'A German' woman owns more than **2,000 clown-related items.**

Halloween started as a Celtic festival known as **SAMHAIN,** a day when the **DEAD** supposedly **RETURNED** to Earth.

146

ASTRONAUTS ONBOARD THE INTERNATIONAL SPACE STATION RECENTLY DRESSED UP AS **ELVIS PRESLEY, DARTH VADER,** AND A **MAD SCIENTIST.**

Candle flames are always shaped like a **TEARDROP.**

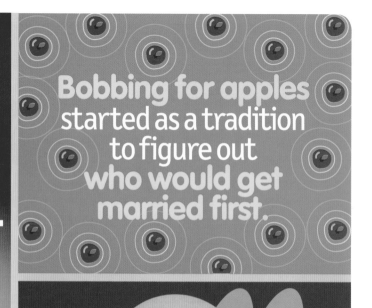

Bobbing for apples started as a tradition to figure out who would get married first.

People used to **LEAVE FOOD OUTSIDE** their houses during Halloween festivals to appease **WANDERING SPIRITS.**

A vampire? Little ol' me?

Instead of **antlers,** male Siberian musk deer— also known as **vampire deer—** grow **vampire-like fangs.**

William Shakespeare's play *MACBETH* includes a recipe for a potion to make in a **WITCHES' CAULDRON.**

Runners in the **Great Pumpkin Haul** in Littleton, Colorado, U.S.A., race while **carrying pumpkins.**

A pumpkin is a **FRUIT,** not a vegetable.

This is getting tricky ...

During a special Halloween event, you can **solve a mystery** and have a **sleepover** at the National Museum of American History in Washington, D.C.

Mount Rushmore

WAS COMPLETED ON

Halloween

IN 1941.

Tennis great

VENUS WILLIAMS

made her

PRO DEBUT

on Halloween in 1994.

A survey found that 7 percent of **cat owners** dress up their cats as hot dogs on Halloween.

Very funny ...

Goblin sharks look pink because their

During Halloween in Jamestown, California, U.S.A., passengers can go for a

blood vessels are visible
through their skin.

"HAUNTED" TRAIN RIDE
with a costumed crew.

White chocolate is NOT ACTUALLY CHOCOLATE; it lacks cocoa solids.

M&M's are named after the two businessmen— Forrest Mars and Bruce Murrie— who started the candy company.

Hundreds of **"WITCHES"** and **"WIZARDS"** **PADDLEBOARD** on the Willamette River in Portland, Oregon, U.S.A., to **CELEBRATE HALLOWEEN.**

The Halloween storms of 2003 were some of the MOST POWERFUL **SOLAR STORMS** EVER RECORDED, causing a power outage in Sweden and rerouted airplane flights.

Flowing veils of gas and dust in the Cassiopeia constellation are nicknamed the ghost nebula.

159

A **SCIENTIST** works behind the scenes at a Pittsburgh, Pennsylvania, U.S.A., **HAUNTED HOUSE** to **STUDY** people's **RESPONSE TO FEAR.**

When you get **scared,** your **pupils dilate.**

Runners **dodge zombies** during a **Halloween race** in St. Louis, Missouri, U.S.A.

You can
SPEND THE NIGHT
and hear a
spooky bedtime
story in a re-created
**ALCATRAZ
JAIL CELL
ON HALLOWEEN
NIGHT**
in San Francisco,
California, U.S.A.

In old skulls, just the BRIDGE remains of the NOSE—it's the only part made of bone.

TEETH are the hardest part of the skeletal system.

CANDY CORN was originally called **CHICKEN FEED** when it was first made more than **100 YEARS AGO.**

You can buy a car **DECAL** that makes it look like **A ZOMBIE** IS WAVING FROM THE BACK SEAT.

The day after **Halloween** is called **All Hallows' Day.**

In
October 2014,
solar activity
on the sun
gave it
the appearance
of a scary
jack-o'-lantern.

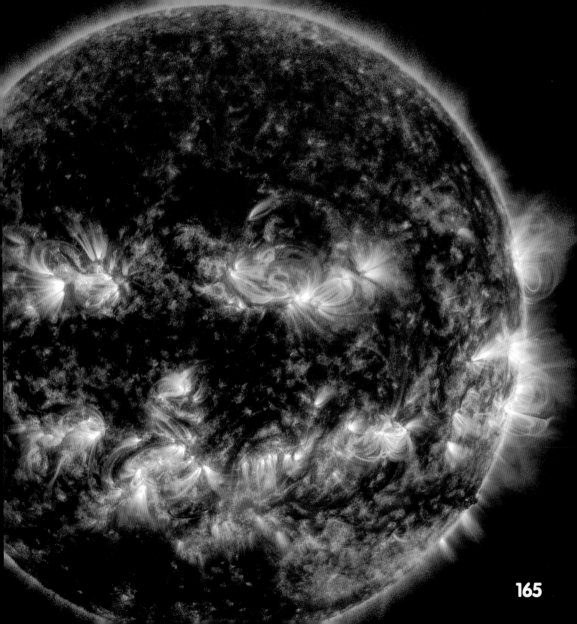

In the Victorian era, "safety coffins" were designed to save people who worried about being

CLIMATE CHANGE is causing leaves to change color LATER IN THE FALL.

Two vials, each supposedly containing A HUMAN SPIRIT, were SOLD in New Zealand in 2010 for MORE THAN $1,500.

BURIED ALIVE.

Vampire finches
peck at the skin of larger birds and **drink their blood** to survive during droughts.

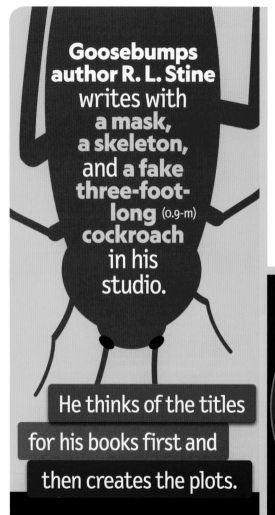

Goosebumps author R. L. Stine writes with **a mask, a skeleton,** and **a fake three-foot-long** (0.9-m) **cockroach** in his studio.

He thinks of the titles for his books first and then creates the plots.

In Old English, the word **"witch"** sometimes meant a **wise woman.**

NASA released a Halloween playlist of **SPOOKY RADIO EMISSIONS** picked up by spacecraft.

I knew they saw me!

A recent study found that nearly **HALF OF AMERICANS BELIEVE** in **GHOSTS.**

In the 1950s, a group of U.S. senators proposed that **OCTOBER 31** be changed to **"Youth Honor Day,"** on which kids would pledge **GOOD BEHAVIOR.**

Americans spent **NINE BILLION DOLLARS** on Halloween in 2018, enough to buy four **PRO BASKETBALL TEAMS.**

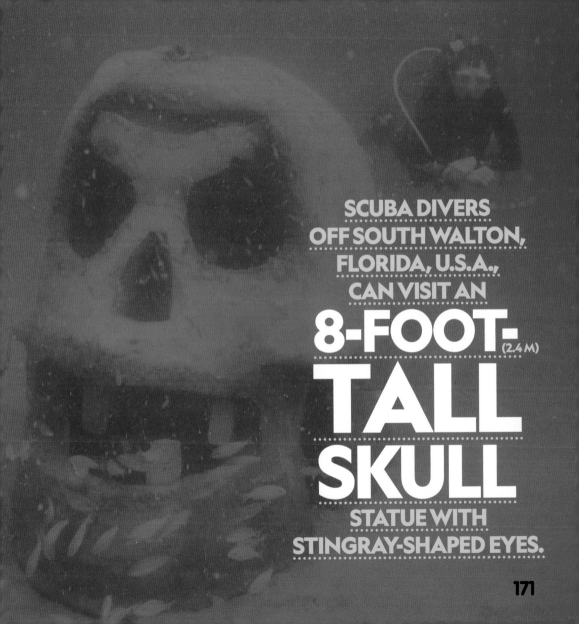

SCUBA DIVERS
OFF SOUTH WALTON,
FLORIDA, U.S.A.,
CAN VISIT AN

8-FOOT-
(2.4 M)
TALL
SKULL

STATUE WITH
STINGRAY-SHAPED EYES.

To maintain a **CREEPY LOOK,** cobwebs that gather in **DISNEYLAND'S HAUNTED MANSION** ride aren't swept away.

During the holiday season, animated **MAN-EATING WREATHS** and **VAMPIRE TEDDY BEARS** are added to the Haunted Mansion.

A **BOARD GAME** is modeled after Disney World's Haunted Mansion attraction.

In New England, the night before Halloween is called **Cabbage Night.** Pranksters collect **rotten vegetables** and leave them on people's doorsteps.

174

THERE IS NO PUMPKIN IN PUMPKIN SPICE.

FOR A PUMPKIN-CARVING CONTEST AT NASA, ENGINEERS MADE A PUMPKIN WITH A ROBOTIC ARM THAT COULD FLIP A LIGHT SWITCH ON AND OFF.

SOUTH CAROLINA, U.S.A., HAS A TOWN NAMED Pumpkintown AND ANOTHER NAMED Spiderweb.

At the Stanley Hotel in Colorado, U.S.A., guests can stay in one of the **"SPIRITED" ROOMS,** which are said to have high **PARANORMAL ACTIVITY.**

A **GHOST** reportedly showed up in a tourist's **PHOTOGRAPH** taken at the hotel.

A farm in Croaker, Virginia, U.S.A., is home to a **"GRAVEYARD"** of **43 GIANT STATUES** of U.S. presidents.

At the **BEN & JERRY'S** **FLAVOR GRAVEYARD** in Vermont, U.S.A., you can visit tombstones of ice-cream flavors that the company no longer sells.

Male **vampire moths** stick their hook-shaped tongue under people's skin and **drink blood.**

VAMPIROLOGY IS THE STUDY OF **VAMPIRES.**

THE PHRASE **"TRICK-OR-TREAT"** WAS FIRST USED IN **1927.**

A candy company set up a **VENDING MACHINE** in New York City where trick-or-treaters could trade in **UNWANTED CANDY** for peanut butter cups.

The world's HEAVIEST PUMPKIN weighed

2,624.6 POUNDS— (1,190.49 kg)

2,624.6 POUNDS
1,190.49 kg

more than a
SMALL CAR!

1,610 POUNDS
730 kg

In some Balkan tales, **WEREWOLVES WERE SOMETIMES KIND** and brought people **TREASURES.**

IN 2008, **PRANKSTERS** DECORATED A NEW YORK CITY SUBWAY CAR AS A **HAUNTED HOUSE.**

On Halloween, some English children carve "**punkies**" out of large beets and then sing the "**Punkie Song.**"

Colcannon—

mashed potatoes with kale or cabbage— is a traditional Irish dish for Halloween.

A coin, rag, and stick are mixed in, and whichever you get is said to **predict your future.**

According
to legend,
you could
BECOME A WEREWOLF by **GETTING BITTEN BY ONE,** drinking water out of a werewolf's footprint, or sleeping outside under a full moon.

You can **jump** in a **bounce house** shaped like a **jack-o'-lantern.**

DINOSAUR GOURDS

get their name from their bumpy outer layer and long neck.

One man set a record by

CARVING A PUMPKIN—

including eyes, nose, ears, and mouth—

IN 16.47 SECONDS.

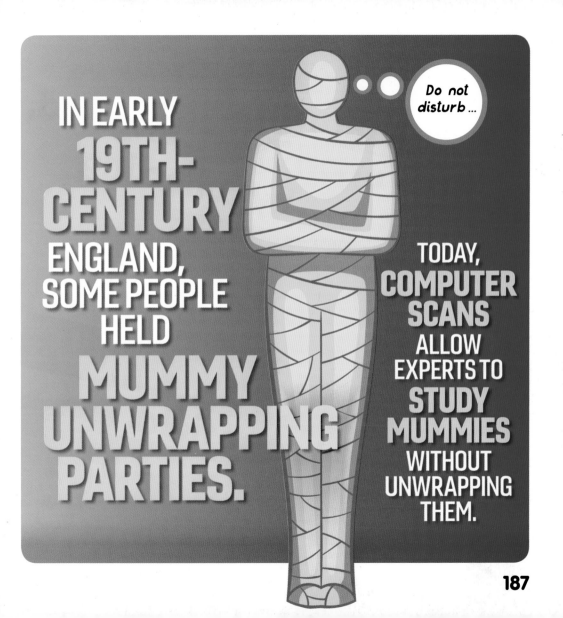

A farm in Burton upon Trent, England, set a record by collecting

3,812

DECORATED SCARECROWS

in one field.

Too late.

Rubbing a pumpkin with **vegetable oil** after it's been carved helps slow down the **rotting process.**

On Halloween in 2000, the first crew to **live on the International Space Station** blasted off from Kazakhstan.

At the Great Jack O'Lantern Blaze in New York State, U.S.A., you can walk through a PUMPKIN PLANETARIUM— a constellation of carved pumpkins that mimics the night sky.

DRACULA ORCHIDS
GET THEIR NAME FROM THEIR
BLOOD-RED PETALS.

The man who invented the

Ouija board

is buried beneath a **tombstone replica** of the game.

NEVADA
BECAME THE 36TH U.S. STATE ON HALLOWEEN IN 1864.

Long-necked **GOURDS** can be used as **BIRDHOUSES.**

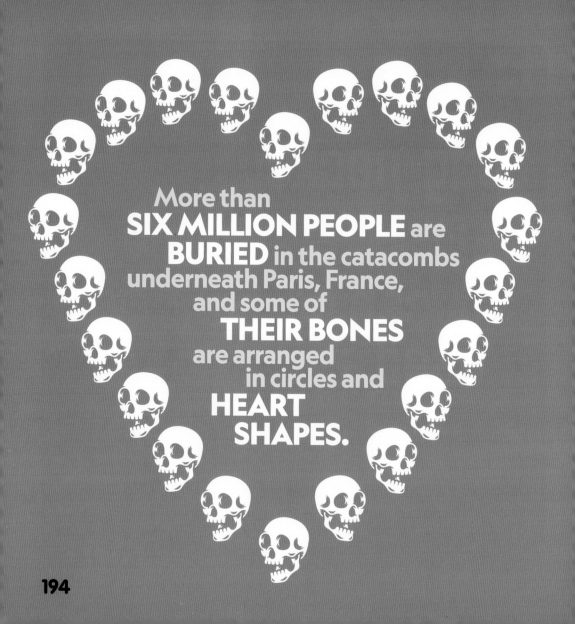

More than **SIX MILLION PEOPLE** are **BURIED** in the catacombs underneath Paris, France, and some of **THEIR BONES** are arranged in circles and **HEART SHAPES.**

White, smooth **nest-egg gourds** are sometimes used to **trick hens** into **laying eggs** in nesting boxes.

In Utah, U.S.A., **a pumpkin** was shot from an

(1,690 m)

air cannon **5,545 feet—**

WISCONSIN, U.S.A., CONTAINS MORE GHOSTS PER SQUARE MILE THAN ANY OTHER STATE, ACCORDING TO ONE AUTHOR.

that's more than **six times** the length of a football field.

In Ireland, objects are **BAKED INTO A CAKE** to foretell fortunes for Halloween—

FINDING A RING means you will marry, but

FINDING A STICK means you won't.

MORE PEOPLE TAKE PART IN HALLOWEEN FESTIVITIES IN THE UNITED STATES THAN LIVE IN JAPAN.

Pumpkin Rock in Norco, California, U.S.A., is about 15 feet tall (5 m) and painted like a jack-o'-lantern.

Boo!

The pale brown Atlantic **GHOST CRAB** has a striking pair of **WHITE CLAWS.**

One of the most common orientations for a grave is facing east, so the **DECEASED "GETS UP"** to face the **RISING SUN.**

Thomas Edison produced the first movie version of *Frankenstein.*

HALLOWEEN is also National Knock-Knock Knock Joke Day.

201

FACTFINDER

Boldface indicates illustrations.

Since 1888, the National Geographic Society has funded more than 12,000 research, exploration, and preservation projects around the world. The Society receives funds from National Geographic Partners, LLC, funded in part by your purchase. A portion of the proceeds from this book supports this vital work. To learn more, visit natgeo.com/info.

NATIONAL GEOGRAPHIC and Yellow Border Design are trademarks of the National Geographic Society, used under license.

For more information, visit nationalgeographic.com, call 1-877-873-6846, or write to the following address:

National Geographic Partners
1145 17th Street N.W.
Washington, D.C. 20036-4688 U.S.A.

Visit us online at nationalgeographic.com/books

For librarians and teachers: nationalgeographic .com/books/librarians-and-educators

More for kids from National Geographic: natgeokids.com

For rights or permissions inquiries, please contact National Geographic Books Subsidiary Rights: bookrights@natgeo.com

National Geographic Kids magazine inspires children to explore their world with fun yet educational articles on animals, science, nature, and more. Using fresh storytelling and amazing photography, *Nat Geo Kids* shows kids ages 6 to 14 the fascinating truth about the world—and why they should care. **kids.nationalgeographic.com/subscribe**

Cover designed by Julide Dengel
Designed by Chad Tomlinson

Names: Beer, Julie, author.
Title: Halloween / Julie Beer.
Description: Washington : National Geographic Kids, 2020. | Series: Weird but true! | Includes index. | Audience: Ages 8-12 | Audience: Grades 4-6 | Summary: "Funny facts and information about Halloween, for kids"-- Provided by publisher.
Identifiers: LCCN 2019034695 | ISBN 9781426338281 (paperback) | ISBN 9781426338298 (library binding)
Subjects: LCSH: Halloween--Juvenile literature. | Halloween--Miscellanea--Juvenile literature.
Classification: LCC GT4965 .B44 2020 | DDC 394.2646-- dc23
LC record available at https://lccn.loc.gov /2019034695

The publisher would like to thank Julie Beer, author and researcher; Michelle Harris, author and researcher; Grace Hill Smith, project manager; Paige Towler and Kathryn Williams, project editors; Julide Dengel, art director; Hillary Leo and Sarah J. Mock, photo editors; Molly Reid, production editor; and Anne LeongSon and Gus Tello, production assistants.

Printed in Hong Kong
20/PPHK/1

PHOTO CREDITS

Abbreviations: AL = Alamy Stock Photo; AS = Adobe Stock; DS = Dreamstime; GI = Getty Images; SS = Shutterstock

Cover: (BACKGROUND), Cattallina/AS; (UP RT), SP Vector Art/SS; (LO LE), martin garnham/SS; (CTR LE), Barbara Helgason/AS; spine: (cat), Martin garnham/SS; (hat), Barbara Helgason/AS; back cover, aalto/AS;1, SP Vector Art/SS; 2, Tartila/AS; 2-3 (BACKGROUND), Cattallina/AS; 3 (UP RT), SP Vector Art/SS; 3 (LO LE), martin garnham/SS; 3 (CTR LE), Barbara Helgason/AS; 5, Willee Cole/AS; 6 (LE), Isselee/DS; 6 (RT), anna_yakovets/AS; 7 (UP), Eric Isselée/AS; 8 (BACKGROUND), Arsen Matevosian/SS; 8, Beth Ruggiero-York/SS; 10, Lowe Family Farmstead, Kuna, Idaho; 12, adisa/AS; 13 (UP), maxsol7/AS; 13 (LO), Bezvershenko/AS; 14, fivespots/SS; 16 (INSET), Magi Bagi/SS; 17 (RT), Courtesy Vat19; 18, Eric Isselée/AS; 19 (UP), ibom/AS; 19 (LO), alestraza/AS; 20 (BACKGROUND), V_ctoria/SS; 20 (RT), Stephanie Pokorny; 21, Kirby Birk; 23 (LE), apple2499/SS; 23 (RT), MrPreecha/AS; 24 (LO), yurakp/AS; 25, FCerez/AL; 26 (LE), mazura1989/SS; 26 (RT), Treter/AS; 27, LI Cook/SS; 28 (LE), ablokhin/AS; 29, Jean Marie Smith; 30, Chalermchai Chamnanyon/SS; 31, City of Santa Rosa; 32, Geza Farkas/SS; 34, Robert Hamilton/AL; 35 (LE), r2dpr/SS; 37, Nathan Pryor; 38, radub85/AS; 40 (RT), LenaBelkin/SS; 41, Tom Leonard/Condé Nast via GI; 41 (ghosts), Tartila/AS; 42-43 (ALL), Timothy A. Clary/AFP via GI; 44 (ALL), Jürgen Otto; 46, Natee K Jindakum/SS; 47 (UP), topvectors/AS; 47 (LO), Courtesy of the NOAA Office of Ocean Exploration and Research, Hohonu Moana 2016; 48 (UP), Yevhenii/AS; 48 (LO), rudall30/SS; 50 (LE), Wilton Brands, LLC; 50 (cat), Kolesnikov Vladimir/SS; 51, Tijana/AS; 52, SuperStock/AL; 54 (LE), Jacky Co/SS; 54 (RT), iuneWind/AS; 55, Vlad Limir Berevoianu/DS; 56 (UP), melazerg/AS; 57, Sviatoslav Kovtun/AS; 58-59, (ALL) Tod Seelie Photography; 60 (LO), Klara Viskova/AS; 61, Courtesy Everett Collection; 62, Pete Niesen/AL; 63 (UP), Irina Silayeva/AS; 65 (UP), Reuters/Toru Hanai Tpx Images Of The Day/Newscom; 66-67, Allan Baxter/GI; 66 (ghosts), tartila/AS; 69 (LO), Zoroasto/SS; 71, Library of Congress Prints and Photographs Division; 72, SimplyFactory/AS; 73 (UP), stournsaeh/SS; 73 (LO), Parinya/SS; 74-75, gregl87/AS; 76, New England Aquarium; 77 (RT), Studio KIWI/SS; 78, Sinelev/SS; 79, Naowarat/SS; 81, Mike Fouque/AS; 82 (LO), Tomasz Klejdysz/SS; 83 (LO), pamela_d_mcadams/AS; 84-85, Maite H. Mateo/VIEWpress/Corbis via Getty Image; 86-87, James Kirkikis/age fotostock; 88, Reimar/SS; 89, SP-Photo/SS; 90, Warner Bros. Pictures/courtesy Everett Collection; 91 (LE), littleartvector/AS; 91 (RT), alexey_ds/GI; 92-93, Treinen Farm; 94 (RT), seanlockephotography/AS; 95 (BACKGROUND), N.MacTavish/SS; 95 (RT), vectorpouch/AS; 96 (LE), partyvector/AS; 96 (RT), Svetislav1944/SS; 97 (UP), Sergio Delle Vedove/SS; 97 (LO), Nomad_Soul/AS; 98, NASA/STScI Digitized Sky Survey/Noel Carboni; 99 (UP), Oxy_gen/SS; 99 (LO), Erik Freeland/CORBIS SABA/Corbis via GI/GI; 100, Annette Shaff/SS; 101, Courtesy Chewy; 102 (UP), Noel V. Baebler/SS; 102 (LO), Steen Drozd Lund/Biosphoto; 105 (UP), freshidea/AS; 105 (LO), New Africa/SS; 106, Forgem/AS; 107 (clown), garikprost/AS; 107 (basket), Dukesn/SS; 108 (UP LE), oleg7799/AS; 108 (LO LE), Vladimir Seliverstov/DS; 109 (paper), M. Unal Ozmen/SS; 109 (slash), Ron Dale/AS; 110-111, Neil Harrison/DS; 114, Anna/AS; 114 (faces), vectortatu/AS; 116, girafchik/AS; 117 (UP), Eleos/SS; 117 (mosquito), Formyline/SS; 117 (LO), osoznaniejizni/AS; 118, William Dummitt/GI; 119 (goblin), sudowoodo/AS; 123, Ken Hawkins/ZUMAPRESS.com/Newscom; 124 (LO), AS; 125, Saul Loeb/AFP via Getty Image; 126, Mindscape Studio/SS; 128 (UP LE), Sleepy Hollow Fire Department; 128 (UP RT), Sergey_Peterman/GI; 128 (LO RT), Mircea Costina/DS; 130, 5second/AS; 131, kzubrycki/GI; 132 (UP), yepifanovahelen/AS; 132 (doll), Bekah93/SS; 132 (tent), mix3r/AS; 133, Courtesy Mark Petryczka; 135 (UP), Maeymay5649/AS; 137 (corn), annarepp/SS; 138-139, rudall30/SS; 142, Klara Viskova/AS; 144 (fish), Iliuta/AS; 144 (UP RT), LanaSham/SS; 146-147, NASA/ESA/Alexander Gerst; 149, suvorovalex/AS; 150, vixenkristy/AS; 151 (UP), HAL Sports/TwainWilkins; 151 (LO), Maksim Pasko/DS; 153, sdominick/GI; 154-155 (UP), Makoto Hirose/e-Photo/BluePlanetArchive; 157, Mark Graves/The Oregonian via AP; 159 (plate), SOMMAI/SS; 159 (spider), Jasius/GI; 160, Adam Hart-Davis/Science Source; 164-165, NASA/GSFC/SDO; 166, Eti Swinford/DS; 167, Pete Oxford/Nature Picture Library; 169, Kit Leong/SS; 170 (LO RT), Lightspring/SS; 171, Cultural Arts Alliance & Spring Run Media; 172-173, Barry King/WireImage/GI; 174, hpoliveira/SS; 175, NASA/JPL-Caltech; 176, p.portal.photo/AL; 176 (ghost), Fotomay/SS; 177, Derivative illustration created by Chad Tomlinson from original by Robert James; 178, FLPA/AL; 180, Christoph Schmidt/dpa/Newscom; 181, arosoft/SS; 182 (UP LE), hadeev/AS; 182 (notes), olegganko/SS; 182 (LO RT), Valentina R./AS; 183 (CTR LE), Kyselova Inna/SS; 183 (UP RT), STILLFX/SS; 183 (CTR RT), Kim Nguyen/SS; 184, Tanakax3/SS; 185 (UP), melissamn/SS; 185 (LO), MarekPhotoDesign/AS; 187, ylivdesign/AS; 188-189, National Forest Adventure Farm; 190, Erin Cadigan/AS; 191, Historic Hudson Valley Tourism; 192 (LE), Morley Read/Nature Picture Library; 192 (RT), croisy/AS; 193, Richard Ellis/AL; 194, Mukhlis santoso utomo/SS; 196 (ghosts), Alena Shenbel/SS; 198, Kris Clifford/SS; 199, Konstantin L/AS; 201, otsphoto/AS

DARE YA!

If you like ghost stories, haunted houses, and other spooky, kooky phenomena, check out this frightfully fun book! Help solve the mysteries surrounding these true tales of strange people, places, and events, and check this out—the Fright-o-Meter ranks each story's scariness from 1 to 10.

NATIONAL GEOGRAPHIC KiDS

DON'T READ THIS BOOK Before Bed

Thrills, Chills, and HAUNTINGLY TRUE STORIES

ANNA CLAYBOURNE